The Story
of Garfield

Also from Westphalia Press
westphaliapress.org

The Story of Garfield

Farm-Boy, Soldier, and President

by William G. Rutherford

WESTPHALIA PRESS
An imprint of Policy Studies Organization

Westphalia Press
An imprint of Policy Studies Organization
1527 New Hampshire Ave., NW
Washington, D.C. 20036
info@ipsonet.org

ISBN-13: 978-1-63391-416-2
ISBN-10: 1-63391-416-X

Cover design by Jeffrey Barnes:
jbarnesbook.design

Daniel Gutierrez-Sandoval, Executive Director
PSO and Westphalia Press

Updated material and comments on this edition
can be found at the Westphalia Press website:
www.westphaliapress.org

JAMES GARFIELD.

Born—
19TH NOVEMBER 1831.

Died—
19TH SEPTEMBER 1881.

THE

STORY OF GARFIELD

FARM-BOY, SOLDIER, AND PRESIDENT

By WILLIAM G. RUTHERFORD

THIRTY-FOURTH THOUSAND

THE WHITE HOUSE

THE NATIONAL SUNDAY SCHOOL UNION

57 & 59 LUDGATE HILL, LONDON, E.C. 4

CONTENTS.

———+———

LIST OF ILLUSTRATIONS.

THE STORY OF GARFIELD.

CHAPTER I.

THE FAR WEST.

The United States Sixty Years ago—The "Queen City" of the West
—The Rush for New Lands—Marvellous Growth of American
Cities.

O to Liverpool or Glasgow, and embark
on one of the great ocean steamers,
which are constantly crossing the
Atlantic. Sail westwards for about a
week, and you will reach the eastern shores of the New
World.

If you land at New York, you will find yourself in
one of the largest cities on the face of the globe. You
will also find the country largely peopled by the same
race as yourself, and everywhere you will be addressed

in your own language. You may travel for weeks
from town to town, and from city to city, until you are
lost in wonder at the vast and populous empire which
English-speaking people have founded and built up on
the other side of the Atlantic.

Where is the New World of fancy and fiction so
graphically described in Indian stories and tales of
backwoods life ?   And where are the vast prairies and
almost boundless forests of sober fact, where the bear,
the wolf, and the buffalo roamed at will—the famous
hunting-grounds of the Red Indians and the trappers of
the Old World ?

Where is the "Far West" of song and story ?
Where are the scenes of Fenimore Cooper's charming
descriptions, which have thrown a halo of romance over
the homes of the early settlers who first explored those
unknown regions ?

For the most part they are gone for ever, as they
appeared to the eyes of the pioneers and pathfinders,
who wandered for weeks through the wilderness, without hearing the sound of any human voice but their
own.   Now on forest and prairie land stand great cities,
equal in population and wealth to many famous places,
which were grey with age before the New World was
discovered.   The trading posts, once scattered over a
wide region, where Indians and white hunters met to
barter the skins of animals for fire-water and gun-

powder, have disappeared before the advances of
civilisation, and the uninhabited wilderness of fifty
years ago has become the centre of busy industries of
world-wide fame and importance.

Sixty years ago, fifteen of the largest cities in the
United States had no existence. They were not
born. Living men remember when they were first
staked out on the unbroken prairie, and the woods-
man's axe was busy clearing the ground for the log
huts of the first settlers who founded the cities of
to-day.

At that period, Chicago, now a "Millionaire city," and
the second in America, consisted of a little fort and a
few log huts. There was scarcely a white woman in
the settlement, and no roads had been constructed.
The ground on which the great city now stands could
have been bought for the sum now demanded for a few
square feet in one of its busy streets.

No wonder the American people are proud of "the
Queen City of the West." It stands far inland, a
thousand miles from the ocean, and yet it is an important port on the shores of Lake Michigan, and steamers
from London can land their cargoes at its quays. More
than twenty thousand vessels enter and leave the port
in one year. It is the greatest grain and provision
market in the world.

It may with truth be said that in America cities rise

up almost in a night-time. The forest and the prairie
are one day out of the reach of civilisation, and the
next they are one with the throbbing centres of life and
progress. The railway, the means of communication,
changes all as by a wizard's touch.

One day the news spread through a certain district,
that two lines of railway were to cross at a certain
point in the wilderness. Settlers at once crowded to
the place, and next day the land was staked out in town
lots, with all the details of streets, squares, and market-
place. Soon afterwards, shanties were seen on the
prairies, moving with all speed, on rollers, towards the
new town. On the second day a number of houses
were under construction, while the owners camped near
by in tents. In a few months hundreds of dwellings
had been erected, and a newspaper established to
chronicle the doings of the inhabitants.

"The old nations of the earth creep on at snail's
pace: the Republic thunders past with the rush of
an express," says a recent American writer. "Think
of it!" he continues; "a Great Britain and Ireland
called forth from the wilderness, as if by magic,
in less than the span of a man's few days upon
earth."

This marvellous growth and rapid change from
wilderness to cultivation must be known and understood by readers on this side of the Atlantic,

they can appreciate the story of a Lincoln or a Garfield who began life in a log hut in a backwoods settlement in the Far West, and made their way to the White House, the residence of the ruler of an empire as large as the whole of Europe.

CHAPTER II.

A New England Village—Hardships of Emigrants—The Widow Ballou and her Daughter Eliza — The Humble Dwelling of Abram Garfield—The Garfields and the Boyntons--The Removal to a New Home—The Wonderful Baby-Boy.

HE early settlers from the Old World first peopled the eastern shores of the Atlantic, and founded the New England States, New York State, and the whole seaboard from Maine to Florida.

A New England village was a collection of log houses on the edge of a deep forest. Snow drifted into the room through the cracks in the walls, and the howling of wolves made night hideous around them. The children were taught in log schoolhouses, and the people worshipped in log churches.

Savage Indians kept the settlers in a state of continual fear. Sometimes they would suddenly surround a solitary house, kill all the inmates, and set fire to the dwelling. Again and again have the children been aroused from their sleep by the fearful Indian war-whoop, which was more dreaded than the howling of the wolves. Even women learned to use guns and other weapons, that they might be able to defend their homes from these savage assaults.

The log house villages grew into populous places, and the descendants of the "Pilgrims" were not always satisfied to remain in the cities founded by their fore-fathers. Wonderful stories were told in the towns of the amazing fruitfulness of the forest and prairie land out West, which induced large numbers to sell their property and set out on the tedious and adventurous journey.

Before the great lines of railway were constructed, which now stretch across the North American continent from the Atlantic to the Pacific, there was a constant stream of emigration from the East to the West. Large waggons carried the women and children, and the stores of necessary articles, which must be conveyed at all cost, for they could not be obtained in the localities to which the pioneers bent their steps.

Slowly the emigrant trains made their way through roadless regions. They had to ford rivers, wade through swamps, and cut paths through thick forests. Weeks, and even months, were spent on journeys which are now accomplished in less than twenty-four hours.

Numerous difficulties and manifold dangers beset the wanderers' path ; yet, regardless of both, they pushed on with infinite courage and patience. Nor was the journey through the wilds without a tinge of romance to the younger and more adventurous spirits, who enjoyed the freedom they could not have in the towns and cities.

About eighty years ago, a widow and her family—a son and a daughter — packed up all their worldly possessions in an emigrant waggon, and started for the West. Widow Ballou made her home in the State of Ohio, which at that time was only peopled by a few scattered settlers. Five years afterwards, a young man named Abram Garfield started on the same journey. It is said that he was more anxious to renew his acquaintance with the Ballou family than to make his fortune. The widow's daughter Eliza was the attraction that drew him into the Western wilds.

On the third of February 1821, Abram Garfield and Eliza Ballou became man and wife, and their first home was a log cabin, which the young husband erected at Newburg, near Cleveland. It was an isolated spot, for Cleveland, the larger place, then consisted of a few log cabins, containing a population of about one hundred persons.

The humble dwelling of Abram Garfield and his young wife had but one large room. The three windows

were of greased paper, a substitute for glass, and
the furniture was home made and of the rudest de-
scription.   Wood was the chief material used.   There
were wooden stools, a wooden bed, and wooden plates
and dishes.   A frying-pan, an iron pot, and a kettle,
made up the list of utensils which were absolutely
necessary.

Nine years passed away, during which the young
couple were very happy in each other's love, and three
children were added to their little family circle.   Abram
worked on the land, and was for a time employed in the
construction of the Ohio and Pennsylvanian Canal.   To
provide for his growing family, the young husband then
bought fifty acres of land, a few miles away from his
first home.   At the same time, Amos Boynton, who had
married Mrs. Garfield's sister, also bought a tract of
land in the same locality.

The two families removed to the new scene of their
labours at the same time, and lived together in one log
cabin, until they had erected a second dwelling.   When
this was done, the Garfields and the Boyntons settled
down to reclaim the wilderness.   They had to depend
on each other for society, as their nearest neighbour
lived seven miles away.

Garfield's new home was built of unhewn logs,
notched and laid one upon another, to the height of
twelve feet in front and eight feet behind.   The

2

spaces between the logs were filled with clay and mud, to keep out the wind and the rain. The roof was covered with boards, and the floor was made of logs, each split into two parts and laid the flat side up. A plank door and three small windows completed the primitive dwelling. There was but one large room on the ground floor, twenty by thirty feet, and a loft above, to which access was obtained by a ladder. In the loft were the straw beds on which the children slept.

The land which the pioneers had bought was part of the forest, and was therefore covered with timber. This had to be cleared away before the land could be brought into cultivation. Much hard work and steady application were needed to accomplish this purpose. Abram Garfield was a strong, well-made man, who shrank from no labour, however hard, and boldly faced every difficulty with a stout heart and a determined will. Early and late he toiled on his farm, cheered by the presence of his wife and children, who were all the world to him. The trees fell before his axe, and ere long he had room to sow his first crop. With a thankful heart he saw the grain ripen, and his first harvest was safely gathered in before the winter storms came on.

In January 1830 he removed to his new home, and in November 1831 his fourth child was born. This

THE TREES FELL BEFORE HIS AXE.

baby boy received the name of James Abram Garfield.
Little did the humble backwoodsman dream that the
name he lovingly gave his child would one day be on
the lips of millions of his fellow-countrymen; that it
would rank with those of princes, kings, and emperors;
and that it would be linked for ever with the history
of the United States of America.

CHAPTER III.

The Effects of Prairie Fires—How Abram Garfield saved his Crops—
The sudden Illness and Death of Abram Garfield—The Grave in
the corner of the Wheatfield.

NE of General Sherman's veteran soldiers was once describing a prairie fire. When he had finished his story, he raised himself to his full six feet height, and with flashing eyes said, "If I should ever catch a man firing a prairie or a forest, as God helps me, I would shoot him down in his deed."

No wonder that the old soldier was fired with indignation when he thought of the terrible consequences which often resulted from such thoughtless or wanton proceedings. The loss to settlers is often appalling. The prairies, which in the day-time seem dry, dull, and uninteresting, give place at night to the lurid play of the fire fiend, and the heavens and horizon seem like a furnace. It is a grand, yet awful sight. Cheeks blanch as the wind sweeps its volume towards the observer, or across his track.

Full in the distance is seen the long line of bright flame stretching for miles, with its broad band of dark smoke-clouds above. Often it rages unchecked for miles and miles, where the cabins of the settlers have just been set up. No words can describe, no pencil paint, the look of terror when the settler beholds advancing towards him the devouring element. When it is first seen, all hands turn out, and a desperate attempt is made to overcome the common foe.

Sometimes a counter fire is started, which, proceeding from the settler's log house in the face of the wind, towards the grander coming volume, takes away its force, and leaves it nothing to feed upon. Then it dies away in that direction. In one instance an emigrant was travelling in a close covered waggon, when he was overtaken by the flames. In a moment, horses, family, waggon, and everything were destroyed, and scarcely a vestige remained of what had been.

Abram Garfield had successfully planted his second crop, which was nearly ready for the harvest, when he one day heard the terrible cry, " A fire in the forest." No one knew better than he did the meaning of those fearful words. Not a moment was to be lost, for he saw that it was coming in the direction of his little farm. He had no one to help him but his wife and his two eldest children, but they all set to work to save their home and the ripening crops.

Rapidly they threw up a bank of earth between the fields and the coming fire, and they so far succeeded that it swept round their homestead and continued its progress beyond.

After the long, hard fight with the fire, on a hot day in July, Mr. Garfield sat down on the trunk of a tree to rest. He had, however, conquered one enemy only to fall a victim to another. While sitting resting, and cooling himself in the open air, he caught a chill. That night he awoke in great pain, and his wife thought that he would die before help could be obtained.

In the early morning she sent her daughter Mehetabel for Uncle Boynton, and bade Thomas fetch their nearest neighbour. No doctor lived near, and the friends did all they could for the stricken man. Their efforts were in vain. Gradually he became weaker, and then without a struggle he passed away. His last words to his wife were: "I have planted four saplings in these woods; I must now leave them to your care."

Mrs. Garfield carried her burden of sorrow to that Heavenly Father whom she had learned to trust before the dark cloud of bereavement fell upon her heart and home. But for her confidence in God, and her belief that He would aid her to bring up her fatherless children, she might have given up in despair.

Far from churchyard or cemetery, the widow arranged to bury her dead in the plot of land he had saved from the fire, at the cost of his life. A rough wooden box was made to contain the remains of the brave husband and loving father, and a grave was dug in a corner of the wheatfield. Four or five neighbours, all who lived within a radius of ten miles, attended the funeral, and tried to cheer the hearts of the widow and orphans by sympathetic words and kind and thoughtful actions. Tenderly they bore the body of Abram Garfield to its last resting-place and committed it to the earth, without a prayer except the silent ones which no ear but God's heard.

Then they accompanied the bereaved ones back to their own desolate home. How desolate it was, none who read this book can fully realise. To be alone in the wilderness is an awful experience, which intensified the loss a hundred-fold.

CHAPTER IV.

The Father's Dying Charge—Advised to give up the Farm—A Noble Resolve—Brave little Thomas—A Hard Time of Trial—The Harvest that saved the Family.

MRS. Garfield had no time to nurse her sorrow. She knew that she must be up and doing, for she had to be both father and mother to her children.

"The four saplings" which the dying father had committed to her care were so young that she could scarcely expect much assistance from them.

Winter was fast approaching, and the strong arm of the husband and father would have been severely taxed to supply all the wants of the family. Without the breadwinner there seemed to be nothing before them but starvation. Uncle Boynton was consulted, and he advised his sister-in-law to give up her farm and return to her friends. He said that she could not hope to carry it on alone, and by her unaided efforts support her children.

Mrs. Garfield saw how dark the future was, and yet she could not follow the advice so kindly given. She thought of the lonely grave in the wheatfield, and declared that nothing would induce her to move away from that sacred spot. She felt somehow that she derived comfort and support from the knowledge that she was near the dead husband, who had prepared this home for her and her children. Added to this feeling, there was the self-respect which independence always brings. She saw that if she sold her farm, which was only partly paid for, the money she received would be swallowed up in paying debts, and in the cost of the removal of her family. But this would leave her and her children homeless and penniless, and she decided to remain on the farm.

It was a noble resolve, and came from a brave heart. To remain meant years of hard work, years of patient endurance, years of quiet suffering and numberless privations; yet she calmly faced them all, that she might do her duty to her children, and faithfully discharge the trust imposed upon her. First, she sold a part of her farm, and with the money she paid her debts. Then, asking God to help her, she prepared to fight her way through the difficulties which beset her path.

Her eldest son, Thomas, was only eleven years old

when his father died. Mehetabel, his sister, was twelve, a younger sister was seven, and James was not quite two. Thomas was a brave little fellow, and when his mother spoke to him about the work that would have to be done, he offered to undertake it all. Though a boy in years, he spoke and acted like a man.

TOM BORROWED A HORSE.

That first winter, alone in the backwoods, was a terrible time. Snowstorms swept around the humble dwelling, and wolves howled in the forest during the long winter nights. Often the children lay awake in terror when they heard the fearful cries of the hungry animals, and knew that their brave protector was no longer there to defend them from danger.

As soon as spring came round once more, Thomas borrowed a horse from a neighbour, and went about the farm work as he had seen his father do. With the assistance of his mother and his eldest sister, he planted

wheat, corn, potatoes, and other vegetables. Then his
mother helped him to fence the wheatfield which
contained her husband's grave. With her own hands
she brought wood from the forest and split it up into
rails for that purpose. Then the whole of the cleared
land, in which the log house stood, was fenced, and the
patient workers waited for the harvest.

The waiting time is often the hardest to bear
Slowly but surely their little store of corn grew less
and less. Fearing to run short before the harvest gave
them a fresh supply, Mrs. Garfield carefully measured
their slender stock, and as carefully doled out the daily
allowance which alone would enable them to pull
through.

She had no money to buy more, and therefore she
gave up one meal a day for herself, that her children
might not suffer from hunger. Still she found that
there was barely sufficient, and the devoted mother
took only one meal a day until the harvest gave a fresh
supply.

Nor did her children know that she pinched herself
for their sakes; as far as they knew, she had enough,
and her self-denial was not allowed to throw a shadow
over their young lives, by the thought that their mother
was starving herself that they might not suffer.

A bountiful harvest, in the autumn of 1834, put an
end to the long-continued strain, and from that time

the little household had sufficient food.　When the noble mother saw her table once more well supplied with the necessaries of life, she thanked God for all His goodness and loving-kindness to her little flock.　Her children had indeed been saved from the pain of hunger, but she never lost the deep lines of care and anxiety brought upon her face in those early years of her widowhood.

CHAPTER V.

A RESTLESS SCHOLAR.

An Intelligent Child—The First School—James questions the Teacher
—Mrs. Garfield's Offer—Winning a Prize.

LIZA, this boy will be a scholar some day!" said Abram Garfield when speaking of James to his wife a short time before his death. Even at that early age, for the little fellow was not two years old, his father saw an unusual intelligence manifested, which gave him a high estimate of his baby boy's intellect.

His mother took great delight in telling him Bible stories, and his inquiring mind prompted him to ask many curious questions, which sounded strange coming from one so young. His acquaintance with the stories of Noah and the Flood, Joseph and his coat of many colours, Moses and the Red Sea, and other old Testament incidents, was remarkable,

Often he amused the children by asking questions, some of which none of them could answer. Then his eyes sparkled with delight as he gave the required information. His retentive memory never seemed to be at fault. What he once heard he remembered. The sturdy pioneers, who had turned their backs on towns and cities to make their homes in the wilderness, did not wish their children to grow up in ignorance. The little settlement soon became a village, and the opening of a school was an event of the greatest importance.

Mrs. Garfield heard the news with thankfulness. A school only a mile and a half away was a boon to her and her children. Now they would get the education required to fit them for a useful life. More than this she did not dare to look forward to.

Jimmy was only three years old when the welcome news reached the log cabin. Thomas, who was not thirteen, at once decided that his little brother should go to school. He would have been glad to go as well, but he knew that his time would be fully occupied in digging up the potatoes and harvesting the corn. Never was mother prouder of her son than was Mrs. Garfield of the sturdy lad, who was ready and anxious to fill a father's place to his brother and sisters, at an age when most boys think only of tops and kites.

About this time Jimmy had his first pair of shoes. Thomas was the good fairy who provided them. By doing odd jobs for a neighbour, he earned enough money to pay the shoemaker. As houses were few and far between, it was the custom for the man to live and do his work in the houses of those who employed him. The happy boy had therefore the pleasure of watching the shoemaker at work. He saw the leather cut into shape, and then formed into shoes to fit his feet. Then there came the joy of wearing them, and the satisfaction of being able to run about without fear of treading on a sharp stone or thorn.

Mrs. Garfield was busy with her needle for days before the school opened, preparing the necessary clothing, that her children might appear neat and tidy. And when the day came round, Mehetabel set out with Jimmy on her back, and her younger sister by her side. When they returned, Mrs. Garfield and Thomas eagerly questioned the scholars, who declared that they had had "such a good time." Full of excitement, they described the events of the day, and regarded the twenty-one scholars present as a most astonishing number.

Yet the school was but a log cabin, like the one in which the Garfield family lived. The teacher was a young man, who taught school one part of the year to earn money to pay for his education in the other part.

3

The teacher received a certain sum of money for his work, and the parents of the children took him by turns to board in their houses. James was an apt scholar, and at once began to question the teacher, to the no small amusement of the scholars. When the teacher told him anything, he wanted to know why it was so, and how the teacher knew. And this curiosity extended to the names of the letters of the alphabet.

Winter came, and James pursued his studies at home. The long winter evenings were spent in reading. Lying on the wooden floor, he eagerly read page after page, by the light of the huge log fire which burned on the hearth. Before he was six years old he had read every book within his reach, and wanted more. Wishful to shorten the journey to school, Mrs. Garfield offered to give a piece of land on one corner of her farm, if her neighbours would put up a building on it. Those who lived near welcomed the project, and the schoolhouse was built.

Then she obtained a teacher from New Hampshire, where she was born, and she arranged that he should begin by boarding with them. Then the whole family worked hard to get all the farm work done before he came, that Thomas might take advantage of his presence among them. The new teacher found his pupils, and especially our friend Jimmy, so very restless, that he made the following rule: "Scholars cannot study their lessons and look about the room; therefore gazing about is strictly forbidden."

James did not know that his attention was everywhere, and that he was always on the alert to hear and to see everything that went on, until he had several times been reminded of the rule. Again and again he pleaded that he had forgotten, and bent his eyes on his book, only to lift them again a few minutes afterwards, to look at something which arrested his attention.

At first the teacher did not understand the active, restless mind that kept the boy in a state of perpetual motion, and he was disappointed when he found that the better James obeyed his rule, the slower progress he made. The fact that he had to think about the rule, and the effort he made to be still and attentive to one thing, retarded him more than any involuntary motions would have done. The teacher spoke to Mrs. Garfield about her boy's restlessness, and said that he feared he should not be able to make a scholar of James. She was so much grieved to hear this, that the little fellow burst into tears, and, burying his face in his mother's lap, said, "I will be a good boy! I mean to be a good boy!"

The teacher saw that he had made a mistake, and that, in trying to keep the boy perfectly still, he was cramping his energies and repressing his natural activity of mind and body. From that day the lad made rapid progress, and he finished the term by winning the prize of a New Testament, which had been promised to the scholar who was best in study and behaviour.

CHAPTER VI.

MAN-MAKING.

At Work on the Farm—A Good Mother's Teaching—A School Incident
—The Building of a New School—Bible Lessons—The Garfields'
Motto.

HE Garfield farm provided for many of the wants of the family, but money was needed to provide clothing and books, and to pay the teachers who came from time to time. Thomas, therefore, earned all he could by engaging himself for short periods to any of the neighbours who required help. James attended school before he was four years old, and began to work on the farm when he was only eight. In the absence of Thomas he took his elder brother's place. He chopped wood, milked the cows, and made himself useful in a variety of ways.

Mrs. Garfield was anxious to give Thomas a chance to make his way in the world, and therefore she arranged that James should make himself as perfect as possible in farm work before Thomas was of age. At the same time, she told James that she looked forward to the time when he would be able to take his place as a teacher or a preacher. In the meantime, it was his duty to do the work that lay nearest to his hand. Just as he set himself to learn with all his might, in the same way he went about the work of the farm. When anything had to be done, he said, "I can do it," and he did. He was not always successful at the first attempt, but his self-reliance caused him to peg away in the face of every difficulty and even seeming failure, and he invariably succeeded in the end.

His mother was ever on the watch to help him by her kindly counsels and wise advice. Many an old proverb, which sank deep into the lad's heart and helped to build up his character, first fell on his ears from his mother's lips. She taught him that man's will to do well was rewarded by God's blessing on his labours. The will to do finds the way to do, and God helps the one who does his best.

This was a revelation to James, who thought that God only helped people to be good. His mother opened his eyes to the fact that this meant to be good in everything—"good boys, good men, good workers, good thinkers, good farmers, and good teachers." After that, he regarded God as One who would help him in his daily labour and make all his efforts successful. Or, in other words, he saw clearly the truth of the proverb: "God helps those who help themselves."

Two phases of his character were developed at a very early age, and these, coupled with good natural abilities, made him master of the situation. As we have already seen, he had plenty of self-reliance, the feeling that he could do anything that could be done, and the determination to make the most of himself. Then he was ready-witted, and able to grapple with unexpected emergencies. This will be seen in an incident which took place when he was a boy at school.

One day he was sitting by the side of his cousin, Henry Boynton, when the two lads began to indulge in little tricks with each other. The teacher noticed their inattention, and, when they laughed out a little louder than they had intended, he called out, "James and Henry, lay aside your books and go home, both of you."

They were so little prepared for such a course of action, that for a moment they remained in their seats with very serious looks in their faces. They both knew that the teacher's authority would be supported at home, and that their parents would be grieved, if not angry, at such a wanton breach of the rules of the school, as that of which they had been guilty.

"Don't dilly-dally!" exclaimed the teacher; "go home immediately!"

The boys passed out of the door at once, and sadly turned homewards, wondering how to make the best of the disaster which had befallen them. ·You will remember that the school was built on the Garfield farm, and that therefore it was quite near James's home. The sharp little fellow suddenly thought of this, and off he ran as fast as he could. Without being seen by his mother, he reached home, and started back again to the school. Then, without a word, he slipped inside and took his seat.

Looking up, the teacher saw him sitting there, and, never thinking that his order had been obeyed, he called out in a severe tone of voice, "James, did I not tell you to go home?"

"I have been home," said the boy quite calmly.

"Been home?" replied the teacher, who was at a loss how to deal with the boy's ready wit in getting out of the difficulty.

"Yes, sir," he said, "I have been home. You did not tell me to stay there."

What could the teacher do under such circumstances but tell the boy that he might remain? He saw that James had learned a lesson, and would not again incur the risk of being sent home in disgrace. Unlike many boys, James showed neither a sulky nor a discontented spirit. He knew that the punishment was deserved, and therefore he set about undoing the mischief by prompt obedience, and his ready wit suggested a way out of the trouble.

Before he left home, Thomas was anxious to make his mother as comfortable as possible. When he heard that the people of the district had decided to build a better school, he bought the old one, and removed it. Then he rebuilt it alongside his mother's cabin.

Sunday was regarded by the pioneers as a day of rest, but the younger members of the various families had never even seen a place of worship. Now and then a travelling preacher called at the settlement, and during his brief stay held a service in one of the log cabins or in the schoolhouse. A journey of five or six miles was often taken to be present at such a service. Whole families, in waggons, on horseback, and even on foot, might have been seen wending their way to the place appointed.

The opportunities for public worship were too few to be neglected, and the dwellers in the wilderness set a high value on such occasional ministrations.

Mrs. Garfield eagerly welcomed the preachers of the gospel who passed that way, and was glad to place the best fare her cabin afforded before the earnest men, who braved many dangers, and suffered innumerable inconveniences, to break to the settlers the Bread of

Life. The Bible was the Book of books in the Garfield cabin. Every day it gave the widow and her children the Divine message, and on Sundays Mrs. Garfield never failed to do the duty of teacher and preacher to her little flock.

The reading of God's book every day, and especially on God's day, was her invariable rule, until her children knew more about the contents and the teaching of the sacred volume, than many town children who enjoyed greater privileges and more numerous opportunities.

How and why the Bible was written, were questions which Mrs. Garfield answered as well as she was able. Why men were wicked, and what hindered them from being good, puzzled James. To him it was a great mystery that any one could continue to do wrong when God was always willing to help them to do right.

At this time a great wave of temperance passed over that part of the country; and James at once questioned his mother about the movement. Living so far away from the centres of population, the lad had no opportunity of seeing for himself the terrible evils of drunkenness. As far as it was necessary, his mother told him of the mischief done by strong drink, and how much better it was to have nothing to do with it. Here again the self-reliant boy had a difficulty. Just as he could not understand how men could help being good, neither could he understand how they could continue to drink, when they found that it only ended in ruin. Yet he heard enough to convince him that strong drink was an enemy, and therefore, at the early age of eight, he became a temperance reformer. Little did the patient mother think that her humble efforts at man-making would produce such grand results, and that she was rearing in that lonely cabin one of the noblest characters the world has ever seen.

The motto of the Garfield family was, "Through faith I conquer." That motto was woven into the life of the boy. Pure in spirit, prompt in action, loyal in thought and deed to God and his mother, James came to regard the boy or man who did not dare to do right as the greatest coward of all.

With such a firm foundation to rest upon, we do not wonder that James Garfield's life has been, and will be, an inspiration to many young men on both sides of the Atlantic.

CHAPTER VII.

A New House—Thomas leaves Home—Sorrow at Parting—James left to Manage the Farm—The Value of Experience.

T length Thomas was twenty-one, and the time had come for him to go out into the world and make a way for himself. One thing he at that time desired above all others, and that was to build a better house for his mother.

To do this properly it was necessary to engage a carpenter, who would make the necessary framework. Then Thomas and James would help him to put up the building. But money was needed to carry out the undertaking, and this was the purpose to which Thomas decided to devote his first earnings when he left home.

One day Thomas returned from an expedition in search of work, in high glee. He had obtained employment in the State of Michigan. He had engaged to assist in clearing the forest, that is, in cutting down trees for a man who was about to make a farm. His wages were to be fifty shillings a month. This sum seemed a very large amount to James, who seldom saw much money, and did not know the important part it

SHE DRIED HER TEARS AND ASKED GOD TO SUPPORT HER.

plays in towns and cities. Though Mrs. Garfield knew that it was better, both for the family and for her eldest son, that he should go away and take a place, a man among men, yet she was very anxious that no evil should befall him.

Thomas had been a faithful son and a loving brother. He had been the mainstay of the family since that sad day when the grave in the wheatfield hid from their eyes the remains of the husband and father, who had never spared himself in his efforts to provide for them.

How much she had leaned on her noble son, even she hardly realised, until she saw him preparing to leave her. The loving labours, the strong hand, and the wise counsels of her boy, now a man, would be sorely missed, yet she dried her tears, and asked the God in whom she had trusted to support her in this new trial, and, above all, to be with the lad. If God was with her son, she knew that all would be well, and that he would come unscathed from the world and its temptations. So, smiling through her tears, she bade him God-speed.

To James the parting was no less painful. He had confidence in himself, and manfully made up his mind to fill his brother's place. Yet he could not see the big brother, who was so dear to him, and who had done so much for him, go away without feeling an aching void in his heart. And Thomas—what about him ? Did he lightly step out into the world, and, glad to enjoy a sense of freedom, go on his new path without a thought of those he was leaving behind ? Not so. The man who as a boy often had so nobly filled a father's place was still a son and a brother. He left the log cabin

AN AMERICAN FARMSTEAD.

47

because he knew that by doing so he could the better help the loved ones who remained behind. Every day, every hour, the gentle, loving mother whom he loved best in all the world would in spirit be with him. The clever brother of whom he was so proud would be ever in his thoughts, and the two sisters who had so faithfully performed their part would not be forgotten.

Brave, noble-hearted, hard-working Thomas Garfield! though only known to the world through his more gifted brother, he belongs to that grand army of self-sacrificing spirits who leave a bright and shining track behind them, and who everywhere make the wilderness and the desert place to blossom like the rose.

While Thomas was cutting down trees in Michigan, James was playing the part of "boy farmer" to the satisfaction of all who knew him. He was but twelve years of age, and yet he went about his work like a man. He said that he could take his brother's place, and he did it. Even the neighbours began to speak with admiration of the diligent lad who was trying so earnestly to fill his elder brother's place. James worked cheerfully; he was satisfied to do his best in the position in which he found himself. He was satisfied to remain in that position until he had qualified himself for a better. He had hopes and ambitions about the future, but his whole time and energies were so occupied in doing his best, that he never for one

4

moment felt the unrest which accompanies a discontented spirit.

James did not know the meaning of the word "hardship" in the sense their neighbour used it. Did it mean
hard work? Not to James, for he was able to do it.
Did it mean hard fare? No, for he had enough to
satisfy all his wants. In the companionship of his
mother and sisters, with health and strength, food
and raiment, where was the hardship? That was a
question which James could not answer. He had not
yet seen and coveted the pleasures, the luxuries, nor
even the conveniences of the dwellers in towns. He
had not felt the want of anything he did not possess
or enjoy. Therefore, while he hoped to be such a man
as his mother had often described, he was content to
leave the future to take care of itself, and was only
concerned in making the most of himself in the
present.

The first season that James had alone, when single-
handed he did the work of the farm, was a severe strain
on one so young, but his readiness to plan or invent
some way of meeting difficulties again stood him in
good stead. He found that by exchanging work with
a neighbour he could help both. So he bargained with
a farmer to give him a hand when he had a little
spare time, and the farmer in return agreed to lend
James his oxen when he needed them.

When the end of the season came, James felt that the responsibility he had assumed, and the work he had carried through, had made a man of him. The daily round of necessary toil, and the constant need for careful consideration and foresight, were an invaluable experience and discipline, which nothing else would have given him.

CHAPTER VIII.

HOUSE-BUILDING.

"James must be a Scholar"—Thomas returns Home and builds a New House—A Lesson in Carpentering—The Volume of *Robinson Crusoe*—James eager to Travel.

MRS. Garfield was glad to see James so contented with his work on the farm, but she was not satisfied to think that his life should be spent in cultivating the soil. One day she spoke to him about this, and said that she wished him to become a scholar. He replied that he also had the same desire—in fact, that he should like nothing better—but he did not see how he could obtain the education.

It was this view of the case that troubled his mother. She could not see any way out of the difficulty, and therefore she had once .more to leave her case in the hands of God. He had made a way for them in times past, when human eyes could see no path, and she believed that He would again render the necessary assistance.

It was a happy day in the Garfields' cabin when Thomas returned. James was the first to see him, and with a loud cry of joy he ran off to meet and welcome his brother. Their mother heard that cry, and from her cabin door she saw her two sons approaching hand in hand. They were both speaking at once, and the burden of their conversation was expressed in the first words Thomas spoke to his mother.

"We are going to have a frame house now," he cried.

A moment later they were all inside the cabin together — mother, sons, and daughters, and in the mother's lap lay a handful of gold, which Thomas had placed there. James danced with excitement as he saw the sparkling coins which his brother had earned. Never before had he seen a gold coin, and he had hardly imagined that such a sum could be within the reach of the humble workman.

Mrs. Garfield looked at the little pile on her knee, and then at her son, but she did not utter a single word.

"Why don't you say something?" cried James in his excitement.

Why? Because she was unable to do so. There are feelings too deep for words, and times when we cannot give expression to the intense joys or bitter sorrows that thrill or rend our hearts.

The bitter sorrow she had experienced when her husband was struck down in his early manhood; the intense joy now possessed her soul when she saw this golden token of her eldest son's love and devotion. The gold that was needed to provide a better house for her lay there, and no one knew its value better than she did. But what were the golden coins to the mother, compared with the pure, unselfish, loving spirit of her son? She would not have exchanged that precious filial affection for all the gold that was coined in royal mint.

Relief came when at length the mother's tears fell on the shining coins. Tears indeed! but tears of joy. Never was there a happier woman in the world than was Widow Garfield at that moment.

No time was lost in carrying out the work, for Thomas was eager to get back again to earn more money while there was plenty of employment. When he had arranged with Mr. Treat, the village carpenter, he made a journey to Cleveland with James to obtain lime, nails, and windows.

A few days after, the carpenter came, and, assisted by Thomas and James, he set about his task. James

had never seen a frame house built, and he was as
eager and curious to watch how the work was done
as he had been years before, when the shoemaker
sat in the log cabin and made him his first pair
of shoes.

He not only watched every operation, but eagerly
lent a hand where he
could. Hammer, chisel, and
plane were in turn used
as deftly as if he had
served an apprenticeship to
the trade. He especially
distinguished himself in
planing the boards ready
for the carpenter, who
declared that James was
equal to a trained work-
man. He did the work
well and quickly, and was
so delighted with his success that he called it "fun."

THE CARPENTER SET ABOUT
HIS TASK.

When the frame was ready, the neighbours came
on an appointed day to help to raise it and put it in
position. This was a great day for Mrs. Garfield, who
received the congratulations of her neighbours, and
listened with motherly pride to the words of praise
they bestowed upon the son who had made this pro-

vision for his mother. Nailing on the boards next gave James work thoroughly to his mind. Boys are always fond of driving nails, and James was no exception to the rule.

The new frame house was a great improvement on the log cabin. It contained three rooms on the ground floor, and two above, and it was altogether better finished and more comfortable than the ruder dwelling had been. The building of the new house had been a most enjoyable time to James, and it had also been a valuable experience to the observant lad. He turned it over in his mind for several months, and then he told his mother that he thought he might be able to earn some money by working at the carpenter's trade. She said that he had quite enough to do, but she was willing to let him try.

"Yes, I will try," said James, for he had long ago found out that there was nothing like trying.

An hour later he was in the carpenter's shop. The man gave him a hearty welcome. When he heard the object of the lad's mission, he at once said—

"I shall be glad to give you a job. I like boys who want to help their mothers. I don't like lazy boys, and I know there is not a lazy bone in your body."

James agreed to begin on the following day, and the carpenter gave him a pile of boards to plane. He was to receive a halfpenny for each board; and to his own delight, and the carpenter's astonishment, he planed one hundred the first day, and received four shillings and twopence. Once more was Mrs. Garfield struck dumb. Her feelings of joy and thankfulness could not find expression in words. Was there ever a mother so blessed with devoted sons? Silently the mother clasped her boy in her arms, and in this way showed the love she could not speak.

James continued to spend as much time as he could spare from the farm work in helping the carpenter, and then, when the winter school opened, he once more gave all his attention to his studies. The day after the school closed, the carpenter engaged him to assist in building a barn. This gave him employment until farming began, and he was paid at the rate of two shillings a day.

When the work was done, he received four pounds, and what was worth more, both to him and his worthy mother, the hearty commendation of his employer, who said, as he gave him the money—

" You have earned every penny of it."

About this time James borrowed a copy of *Robinson Crusoe,* which he eagerly devoured. It opened a new world to the lad's inquiring mind, and awakened within him a strong desire to travel and see something of the world.

Two or three incidents of his youth may here be told, as they serve to still further illustrate the different phases of his character.

A friend invited him to make a short excursion to visit an acquaintance on the Sunday. James at once refused. His friend pleaded that it was the only day on which the visit could be made, but James would not be persuaded. He said that it would be against his mother's wishes; therefore, if he never went, he would not go on Sunday.

One day he found the same friend throwing stones at the cat. James at once stopped him, and spoke so earnestly against cruelty to animals that the youth begged pardon for his thoughtless conduct, and said that he should ever afterwards befriend cats. In the school there was a fatherless boy like himself, who had no older brother to stand up for him. When James saw the bigger boys teasing the little fellow, he took the boy's part, and compelled his tormentors to leave him in peace.

The seasons followed each other in rapid succession, and with each came the tasks which gave James the employment he so much enjoyed. The farm, the carpenter's shop, and the school kept him busy, and at fifteen he could do a day's work with any man in the district. Studying geography and reading books of travel had, however, one effect on his mind—they made him eager to see the places about which he had read. When he spoke to his mother on the subject, she expressed a wish for him to remain at home until a fitting opportunity came.

"Wait for Providence," she said; and in the meantime James waited.

CHAPTER IX.

A New Employment—At the Potash Works—Desire for a Seafaring
Life—On a Farm again.

ONE day Farmer Smith called at Mrs.
Garfield's house, to ask James to help
him in weeding the peppermint, add-
ing at the same time, that he had
engaged twenty boys for this especial purpose. Mrs.
Garfield said that her son was at that time very busy,
and she thought that the farmer would have enough
boys without him.

The farmer replied that without James he should
have altogether too many. He had engaged them with
the intention of getting James to lead them, because of
the wonderful influence he had over them. " James,"
said the farmer, " is a fast worker, and all the time he
so interests the boys with stories, anecdotes, and fun,
that they do their best to keep up with him. I am
quite willing," he continued, " to pay James something

extra, and I shall then be the gainer by engaging him."

The farmer had employed James before at similar work, and therefore he knew the value of such an active, cheerful servant. Once more he agreed to take command of the weeders, and the work was again done to the entire satisfaction of the shrewd farmer. The last job in which James helped the carpenter was the building of a shed in connection with a large potash factory. The owner of the works saw him, and noticed how he gave his whole mind to the business in hand. As soon as it was done, he was eager to employ the lad.

When James received an offer of nearly three pounds a month from the manufacturer, he was filled with surprise. It was nearly ten shillings more than was usually paid.

"I want just such a hand as you in my business," said the man; "and you may come as soon as you like, and remain as long as you please."

"I must first consult my mother," said James, "and if she consents, I will begin work on Monday."

Mrs. Garfield was filled with fear when she heard of Mr. Barton's offer. She said that the rate of wages was high, but the workmen who were engaged in the factory were rough and coarse in their speech and manner of life. James replied that he had no fear of being led away by their bad example. He said that evils would meet him everywhere, and that he was quite able to resist all temptation to do wrong. The wise mother did not question the strength of his power to resist evil, but she reminded him of the text, "Let him that thinketh he standeth take heed lest he fall."

Then, when she had sufficiently impressed upon his mind that there was a real need for the utmost care, she gave her consent. Indeed, she could hardly refuse when James reminded her that he was waiting for Providence to open a door, and that if Providence had not opened this door, he should never know when Providence did open one.

James went to the factory on the following Monday morning, and was at once set to keep the books of the establishment, and attend to the buying and the selling of the potash. The manner in which he attended to business caused Mr. Barton to place absolute confidence in him, and to treat him with the utmost kindness. James was the first to enter the factory in the morning, and the last to leave it at night. The men who brought ashes for sale were not always honest, and they often charged for more than they delivered. James, in measuring their loads, soon found out that his master was being systematically robbed. He put an end to such unprincipled conduct, and thereby still further increased Mr. Barton's confidence in him.

At the works, the men were, as his mother had described them to be, rough in manner and very profane
in their conversation. This gave James so much
pain, that he kindly but firmly pointed out the wicked-
ness as well as the uselessness of swearing; and
though he was told that it was no business of his to
take notice of these things, his presence was an influence for good over them.

While living in Barton's house, he read a number
of books on seafaring life and the doings of famous
pirates. They fired his imagination so much, that
he never tired of reading them, and he conceived
a strong desire to be a sailor. This desire became
stronger every day, and when Mr. Barton spoke to
him about settling down to the potash business, James
told him he wanted to go to sea. The old man
spoke strongly against such a course, and told him
that if he would stay in his service, he might look
forward to the time when he would have a factory
of his own.

James was not willing to give up his idea of going
to sea, but he remained for some months with his
employer. One day, however, Mr. Barton's daughter
spoke of him as a hired servant, and this made James
so angry, that, in spite of the persuasions of his master,
he left the factory, and returned home on the following
day.

His mother was glad to see him back again, though she did not agree with his hasty action in leaving without notice. James explained to his mother that he had not taken offence at being called a hired servant, but at the insulting manner in which the words were said. Then he filled her heart with dread by express-

HE NEVER TIRED OF READING.

ing a wish to go to sea. This was a severe blow to his mother, who told him that she could never give her consent to that. She even told him to say no more about taking such a step unless he wanted to make her unhappy.

As a man had been engaged to do the work on Mrs. Garfield's farm, James once more went away in search of a job. This time he was employed by an uncle, who lived at Newburg, to chop wood. While there he lodged with his sister Mehetabel, who had been married some time before. He now worked within sight of Lake Erie, and his desire to be a sailor was intensified when he saw the vessels sailing to and fro on the broad expanse of water before him. At first he lost much time watching the ships, but when he found that his work suffered, he gave it all his attention.

When he spoke to his sister about being a sailor, she replied as her mother had done, and told him that he had better be anything than that. He was too clever, she said, to throw away his abilities on board a ship.

When the work was done, James carried the money he had earned to his mother, and then engaged to help a farmer who lived a few miles away. The work was very hard, and the men were busy from early morning till late at night. James, however, would not be beaten.

"If I can't do as much as others do," he said, "I will give up the job."

At the end of the season he received his wages, and the farmer said, as he paid him, "You've done well."

CHAPTER X.

The Driver of a Canal-boat Mule-team—Defence of the Right—James
speaks out plainly—A Narrow Escape—A Severe Illness—The
Turning-point in James's Life.

WHEN Mrs. Garfield found that James had
become unsettled and restless, she
decided to give way, and allow him to
obtain some experience of a seafaring
life. Finding that he had no definite plan in his
mind, she proposed that he should try a voyage on
Lake Erie.

This suggestion fell in with his wishes, and, once
more taking his bundle in his hand, he set out to seek
his fortune. On foot he journeyed to Cleveland, a
distance of seventeen miles, and went on board the
first vessel he saw. There he inquired for the captain
of the schooner, whom he expected to be a gentleman.
To his disgust, the man who appeared was a drunken,
swearing fellow, who, with a volley of oaths, threatened

to throw him into the dock if he did not at once leave the vessel.

No pleasant dream was ever more rudely dispelled than were James Garfield's bright visions of the charm of a seafaring life. No such wretch as the captain he had just met with had been described in any of the books he had read, and he began to think that there must be a mistake somewhere. At any rate, he had no present intention of giving up the idea of being a sailor. While walking along the side of the docks, he met his cousin, Amos Fletcher, who was the captain of a canal boat, and to whom he related his recent experience.

Amos offered him the post of driver, and James engaged to go with his cousin to Pittsburg in that capacity. His work was to take turns with another driver, and, for a certain number of hours, when his turn came, to drive the two mules which drew the boat along the canal.

The boatmen were profane, coarse, vulgar whisky-drinkers, "who regarded rum and tobacco as among the chief necessaries of life." A greater contrast there could not have been than that which existed between James and the men among whom his lot was cast.

The work required some experience, and the very first day the new driver and his mules were thrown into the canal, while trying to pass another boat. At

once the other men ran to his assistance, and, when
James and his mules were placed safely on the
towing-path, he had to stand a considerable amount of
good-humoured chaffing.

Amos had been engaged in teaching before he became
the captain of a canal boat, and when he found how
much James knew, he spoke very seriously to him
about his future prospects. His cousin told him that
with a little more education he would be well qualified
to take charge of a school, and strongly advised him to
adopt this course. James now remembered that not
only his mother and sister, but every one to whom he
had spoken, had told him he was throwing himself
away in seeking to be a sailor, and therefore the words
of his cousin had considerable influence over him. He
began to think that he had been guilty of acting
foolishly, and to waver in his purpose.

One day the boat came to a lock the same time as
another boat, and the crews of the two vessels were
about to fight for the first turn, when James spoke out
boldly, and declared that the right belonged to the
other boat, and that it should precede them. The
captain was so struck with his cousin's manly defence
of the right, that he ordered his men to give way. A
fight was prevented, and fair play was given to the
first comers. Some of the men in his own crew
called him a coward, but that had no effect on James,

ON BOARD THE CANAL BOAT.

He had long ago settled in his own mind that the greatest coward was the one who did not dare to do right.

Not long afterwards James offended one of the men, who at once set upon him. To save himself, James knocked the man down. All the men at once called upon James to pitch into him while he was on the ground. But James replied that he never struck a man when he was down. This was a new idea to the men, who had called him a coward because he would not fight for that which did not belong to him. Ever afterwards they regarded him with respect. Even they, rough and brutal as they were, could appreciate the generous spirit which prompted such noble actions.

One of the boatmen, named Harry Brown, was a good-hearted fellow, who took a great fancy to James. This man was, however, so very fond of drink, that he was always getting into trouble. James tried to persuade Harry to give up drinking, and the man listened willingly to the kind advice which he found so hard to follow. When speaking of James to one of the crew, Harry said, " Jim is a great fellow. I should like to see what sort of a man he will make. The way he rakes me down on whisky, tobacco, and swearing is a caution, and he does not say a word that is not true. I like him, though. I always like a man to show his colours."

All through life it was the same. No matter where he was, or in what circumstances he was placed, James Garfield always showed his colours, and he was never afraid to nail them to the mast.

Therefore the ignorant, drunken crew not only respected the lad who so boldly reproved them, but boasted of the companionship of one so unlike themselves. Said the steersman to the bowman of another boat, "We have a fellow in our crew who never drinks, smokes, chews, swears, nor fights; but he's a jolly good fellow, strong as a lion, could lick any of us if he has a mind to, and a first-rate worker. I never saw such a boy." Both captain and crew agreed that James was a peacemaker, and that he carried out his purpose without making enemies. Thorough and prompt in everything, and unwilling to be a party to any wrong-doing, he was regarded as a model worthy of imitation by all who knew him.

During the few months that he was on the canal boat, James fell into the water fourteen times. The last time nearly cost him his life. It was a dark and rainy night, and no one saw him jerked into the water. The boat swept on, and just as he began to despair of receiving any aid, his hand caught a rope in the darkness, and he drew himself into a place of safety. He found that the rope that had served his purpose had held fast by catching in a crevice on the edge of the deck. That was all that had come between him and death. Never had James had such serious thoughts in his mind as then, when he saw the rope and how it had saved him.

At once he thought of his praying mother, and the over-ruling Providence in which she so firmly believed. And at that moment he made up his mind to leave the canal boat, and return to his home.

A few weeks afterwards, James was attacked by ague, and he decided to go at once. It was eleven o'clock at night when he reached the house. Looking through the window, he saw his mother by the light of the fire. She was on her knees. Listening for a moment, he heard the words that fell from her lips. She was praying for him. A moment later, mother and son, once more reunited, were sobbing in each other's arms. Then James told his mother all about his life on the canal, and how God had preserved him almost by a miracle from drowning. After that he went to bed, and next day was found to be so ill that he was laid up for several weeks.

During that period Mrs. Garfield often spoke to James about his future, and he agreed with his mother, that if God saved his life on that night, He must have saved him for something. Then she brought her son under the influence of the teacher of their school, who was preparing to be a minister, and he soon showed

James that the difference between a scholar and a sailor is the difference between somebody and nobody.

James decided to continue his education. That was the turning-point in his life. His mother knew that, having once said, "I will go to school," he would keep his word, and from that time she was satisfied.

CHAPTER XL.

James decides to attend a College—He obtains Employment whereby
to pay his Fees—Looking Upward.

I N the life of every strong youth there
comes a time when the manhood
within him awakens to a consciousness
of its proper powers.   Such a moment
had come in the life of young Garfield.

His best friends had striven hard to awaken his
slumbering ambition ; even the companions of the
towpath and of the woodyard had spoken with regret
of the apparent waste of such abilities as he had
shown ; while his mother, who had been the first
to perceive his talents, never ceased to urge her boy to
fit himself for an honourable and useful calling.

All this advice, however, seemed to be thrown away
on the strong-willed youth, until that moment when
the Spirit of God laid hold of him.   Then, as if a lamp
had been lit in the empty house, his whole nature was

transfigured. He was still the same sturdy, happy, self-reliant lad; but he was also a youth with a purpose in life. He no longer allowed passing fancies to rule his conduct, but, fixing his eye upon one goal, he began splendidly to push his way towards the prize upon which he had set his neart.

With a natural shrewdness, he saw at once that a man without culture and mental training could not climb high on the ladder of life. He saw that knowledge was the one key which opened the door to power in America, and with characteristic energy he set himself to seek that key.

The story of Garfield's attempts to gain an education forms one of the most romantic portions of his history. At first the height of his ambition was to attend a little Western college called Geauga Seminary, a school where about a hundred youths and maidens were gathered, under the auspices of the Free-will Baptist denomination, at the town of Chester in the State of Ohio.

Garfield, accompanied by two cousins, arrived at Geauga Seminary on March 5, 1849. It was perhaps the most important moment of his life, when the big, awkward, ill-dressed boy crossed the threshold of that humble college, and began to tread the path that was to lead straight on to one of the highest places of dignity on earth.

He and his companions hired a room, and with but a little in money, a sack or two of provisions, some pots and pans, and an old school-book, began their simple college course.

Garfield's plans to make his money last as long as possible were amazing. He began with about two pounds, his dear mother's savings, but text-books and school fees had already reduced his tiny fortune.

At first the lads did their own cooking, with indifferent success. Next they tried to live on bread and milk, but found it insufficient. Then Garfield discovered a local carpenter who had planks to plane, and in his spare time he found employment with him. Thus, working at his books in the daytime, and toiling at the bench at night, he plodded along. And yet, though his struggles were long and trying, there was no need for pity in the condition of the young student.

Probably no conceivable circumstances would have better developed the character of this backwoods scholar. His hardy limbs found real pleasure in work, which kept his body braced and healthy, while the active mind was exerting its great faculties in the keen pursuit of knowledge.

Some of the most interesting and instructive periods in the lives of the greatest men, both in this country and in America, have been found in just such conditions as these. Thoughtful English lads will

never tire of hearing about those men, who, starting
at the lowest point of mental knowledge and social
opportunities, have yet contrived to fill in their day a
large space in the world of letters. Take for example
the stories of the three cobbler lads—Drew the historian,
Cooper the reformer, and Carey the missionary, who,
each in his own way, proved superior to poverty and
all its attendant disadvantages, and rose, the one from
his bench to a professorship in the London University ,
the other from a position equally lowly to a high place
among the thinkers and writers of his day; and the
third, leaving his lapstone to take up the pen of a
translator, from cobbling boots in a back kitchen, went
out to be the great master missionary of his age.

And just as in olden times God called His chief
servants from the farmstead and the sheep-run, so even
still the men of might have been those whose natures
were made strong by youthful hardship and boyish
battles.

The slave lad who became the Old World's greatest
statesman, the shepherd boy who became its noblest
king, and the young farmer who stood among its
mightiest prophets, are but the types and forerunners
of the Luthers and Lincolns and Garfields of more
modern days.

Garfield, when once his eyes were opened, was quick
enough to see that no boy could possibly succeed in

life while he remained in ignorance. He said over and over again, "Mother, I must have an education"; and, having made up his mind to this, he set himself to secure it in the only possible way.

No false pride hindered him, no difficulties drove him back. He knew that he would have to begin at the bottom, and he knew also that he would have to work his way, every inch of the long journey.

One of his own wise sayings was this: "Poverty is uncomfortable, as I can testify; but, nine times out of ten, the best thing that can happen to a young man is to be tossed overboard, and compelled to sink or swim for himself. In all my acquaintance, I never knew a man to be drowned who was worth saving." ′ No man illustrated his own words better than James Garfield.

> "Labour is glory !—the flying cloud lightens ;
>   Only the waving wing changes and brightens ;
>   Idle hearts only the dark future frightens ;
>   Play the sweet keys, would.t thou keep them in tune."

CHAPTER XII.

First Term at College—The Pleasure of real Success—James Garfield
meets his Wife—He applies for a Schoolmastership—A Generous
Offer.

T is sometimes said that education spoils
lads for hard work. As a teacher in
after years, Garfield had often to argue
this point with the fathers of his pupils,
who feared lest the college should unfit their boys
for the farm and the forest. But better than any
argument was his own example.

His first duty on returning home from school was
to build his mother a new barn. "It spoils some boys
to go to school," said his brother Thomas at the beginning of the first vacation, but it had not spoiled
James Garfield.

With his brother's help, he built the barn, and then
set off to find work among the neighbouring farmers.
Haymaking occupied him for several weeks, then a

few odd jobs continued to fill up his time, until the
school reopened. During the holidays he had earned
enough to pay a doctor's bill, to provide himself with
a new outfit, to help his mother a little, and, last of
all, to return to the school with ninepence in his
pocket—his sole possession with which to face another
term.

It was characteristic of his plucky and unselfish
spirit, that, on the first Sunday after his arrival at
school, Garfield dropped this money into the collection-
box at church, and so stood in his class on the Monday
morning absolutely penniless.

It was during this second term that Garfield
began to develop those powers of a leader and
speaker which afterwards made him famous. He
had a strong sense of discipline, and by his own
example he was able to put down a rising rebellion
in the seminary.

A youth who had been impertinent to a townsman,
and had thus brought the school into disgrace, was
threatened with expulsion. The students called an
indignation meeting, and a large number of them
agreed to leave the school if the offender were expelled.
But Garfield proved a difficulty.

"Why should I leave because Bell is sent away?"
was his question.

"To show your indignation," was the reply.

6

But Garfield did not feel indignant that way. He held that the youth had no right to insult a townsman, and that, if he would be offensive, then he ought to be ready to pay the price of his impertinence. This was rather a new view to some of the protesters ; and when young Garfield added that if the wrong-doer was sorry for his fault, and would apologise for the insult, he would be the first to plead for him with the principal, he carried the day. The lad was forgiven, the rebellion was put down, and the credit of the school was saved.

Perhaps no period of Garfield's life was more crowded with pleasant recollections than the terms he spent at Hiram Institute. It was here that he began to experience the pleasure of real success, and some of the acquaintances made under the roof of this Western college became his fast friends.

Chief among these was a young lady of great personal attractions, and of still more charming character, the daughter of a neighbouring farmer. Miss Lucretia Rudolph was a scholar in the Chester School during the time of Garfield's attendance there. Afterwards she came to Hiram Institute, where the two young students had the privilege of seeing much of each other, and the friendship there formed rapidly ripened into love, and the two were married in November 1858.

It was this moral courage which gave Garfield his great influence over his companions all through life. And when, after his second term at Geauga, he felt himself able to undertake the charge of one of the winter schools, which were started for small settlers' children, it was this quality, above all others, which made him a successful teacher.

He finished his second term at the top of his class. His mental powers were now thoroughly awakened, his mind was quick, his memory retentive, and he soon out-distanced all competitors. Every evening during the session he had found his way into the carpenter's shop, and with such results, that he finished the term in good health, without debt, and with nearly a pound in his pocket.

Now he was resolved to try his hand at "keeping school." But at first he had some difficulty in finding a school to keep. His youthful appearance frightened the managers at one place; they did not want "a boy to teach at their school." His second and third applications were too late; the vacancies were filled up. At the next place he was even more discouraged, for, said the manager, "We had one fellow from Geauga Seminary, and he made such a botch of it, that we don't want another."

As frequently happens, the opportunity came just when hope was lowest. He reached home thoroughly discouraged with these repeated refusals, and almost too hopeless to respond to his mother's kindly, cheerful words. But there was a purpose in all this apparent failure. At his own door lay the task which was to try the metal in the man, and it was here that young Garfield was to prove the master spirit that was in him.

At a place close by, called The Ledge, was a school without a teacher. And next morning one of the members of the committee of management came over to offer the post of master to young Garfield.

James was eager enough to secure a school, yet he hesitated to accept this offer. The Ledge was a district notorious for the roughness of its inhabitants, and for the unruly character of its young people. Besides, many of the youths in this school were old acquaintances of Garfield, and the young teacher naturally shrank from undertaking such a charge.

After duly considering the matter, however, Garfield accepted the post. His pupils were the sons and daughters of the neighbouring farmers, and many of them were quite grown up. They worked on the farm in the summer, and then attended school for a few months in the winter.

Garfield, of course, knew well enough that while

among such a class there were a few like himself, anxious to get an education, a still larger number were quite indifferent, and looked upon the school as a place for unbridled fun. Two previous masters they had already driven out, and the committee had experienced as much difficulty in procuring a master, as Garfield had found in securing a school.

James feared that his scholars, knowing so much of his early history, would be likely to hold both his scholarship and his character somewhat lightly. He found, however, that this acquaintance was really his best recommendation.

His manly, straightforward character had an attraction for them; his skill and strength as an athlete, and his known courage, ensured him the respect even of the most turbulent among his scholars. The lads felt that their master was a boy who was making his way in life; they knew that he was no mere bookworm, but one of themselves, only stronger and abler.

His shrewd native wit saved him from many a mistake. He was prudent and firm, ready and resourceful, and his sharp tongue was a weapon they feared even more than his heavy hand. His wildest scholars admired him; while his sympathy with those pupils who, like himself, possessed no advantages save such as could be gained by their own hands, endeared him to the more thoughtful.

Thus, when his first season as a teacher was ended, he returned home with the reputation of one of the most successful common schoolmasters in the country.

CHAPTER XIII.

The Young Janitor at Hiram Institute—Personal Appearance at this
time—Teaching and Preaching—The Tailor of Troy—The Beginning of the Civil War.

AMES Garfield attended the Geauga
Seminary three years in succession.
During his second and third vacations
he acted as master in some of the log-
schools in his native county.

Then, at the age of twenty, he went from teaching
school to sweeping the college floor at Hiram Institute.
Here, besides gaining a considerable step in his education,
Garfield began to exercise his gifts as a speaker. The
debating society of his college found in him its most
fluent disputant, and the college became immensely
proud of the promising youth, whose reputation as
a ready and effective speaker was spreading far and
wide.

In two ways he found outlet and exercise for the

more generous instincts of his nature—in preaching the Gospel and in denouncing slavery. Even as early as this, the great struggle that was fated to bathe his nation in blood and fire was looming near, and the nobler among the young men of the country were unconsciously preparing to play their great parts in the awful civil war.

On entering Hiram Institute, Garfield was too poor to pay the ordinary fees. He had applied, therefore, for the post of janitor, and his duties were to sweep the rooms and ring the bell. He held this office for one year, and during the whole of that time it was said that never once did his bell ring behind the time.

From the humble position of janitor he was promoted at the end of the session to the more honourable one of assistant tutor. It seemed as if his experience was to be a continual example of the possibility, and even the advantage in some respects, to a healthy lad, of combining great success in study with great industry in manual labour.

His pay as a teacher was little more than nominal, and it was still necessary that he should work to live, therefore he engaged his mornings and evenings, as at Geauga, to a local carpenter, and thus supported himself.

Such perseverance as this of course attracted the attention of both his fellow-students and his professors.

By the former he was voted "a brick," by the latter
he was mentally designated for a future professor and
principal of the Institute; while in the minds of both
young men and old there was a feeling, slowly shaping
itself into a prophecy, that such ability and courage
and character could have but one end, and that Garfield
was destined to become President of the United States.

When he entered the Geauga Seminary, it was
probably with no expectation of proceeding farther
on the road of learning than the limited resources
of that little country college could carry him. His
success there had sent him on to the Hiram Institute,
and now it was a matter of course that he should go
to a university and take his degree. But once more
the money difficulty faced him, and once more the
devotion of one of the best brothers in the world
opened the way. Thomas was doing fairly well as a
farmer; he had saved a little money, and this he
offered as a loan to his brother. James accepted the
loan gladly; and, to secure his generous brother against
loss in case of his own death, he insured his life for
one hundred pounds.

Garfield had acquired none of the outward graces of
fashionable young men when he entered upon his career
at Williams' University. He was tall, big-limbed, and
rather lanky. His garments were of the homeliest
manufacture, and his speech was somewhat broad and

provincial. In mental stature, however,—in scholarship and reading and judgment,—he was a man, every inch of him. His fine face and magnificent head and sparkling eyes gave promise of rare powers, and once more, and with perfect ease, he took his place in the front rank of his fellow-students.

Here, as at each stage in his eventful life, young Garfield proved that every person must decide for himself the amount of respect that is really due to him from his companions.

No one could have entered college with a more homely appearance than Garfield. His rustic manners and still more rustic dress invited criticism among the smart young men of his college, yet because he was by nature a gentleman, he was treated from the first as such, by both teachers and students alike.

His vacations, as before, were spent in teaching, and his Sabbaths in preaching. In this latter office he acquitted himself so well, that it became quite an accepted opinion that he was to become a minister. This was one mark of the high estimation in which he was held, but there were others besides. The position of teacher in a high school, at the handsome salary of two hundred and fifty pounds, was offered him at this time. The offer, however, was declined, for the reason that it would prevent him taking his degree, and thus interfere with his plans in life.

His ambition was a very noble one. He wished, he
said, to take a degree, to win, if possible, a name for
scholarship; and then to go back to the modest salary
and the limited sphere of the Hiram Institute, and
thus help the humble college which had done so much
for him.

Another illustration of the good name he had earned
was shown in a smaller, but still very practical way.
His brother Thomas's resources had unfortunately given
out, and James was in urgent need of money to buy a
suit of clothes. Careless as he was about his personal
appearance, the state of his wardrobe had become a
serious anxiety to him. One day a tailor in Troy sent
for him, took his measure, and fitted him out, saying,
" Go on with your education, and when you have some
money for which you have no other use, pay me." This
was a little matter in itself, but of great interest as
showing the opinion which his neighbours had formed
of the young man.

It was during his residence at Williams' that the
country was thrown into excitement by Preston Brooks'
attack upon Charles Sumner. Sumner had taken a
prominent part in the growing desire of the Northern
States of America for the abolition of slavery. He was
a Senator of the United States, and a politician and
orator of great influence.

One day, as he sat writing at his desk in the Senate

House, two men came up to him.   One of these, a Senator
and a slaveholder from South Carolina, of the name of
Brooks, was armed with a heavy stick.   This ruffian
attacked Sumner from behind, felled him with a blow,
and then beat him as he lay upon the floor, leaving
him almost dead.   For this grievous offence a small
fine was imposed upon Brooks, and the amount was
promptly paid by his admiring constituents.   The bully
then resigned his seat, and was re-elected without
opposition by the South as its spokesman, leader, and
law-maker.

The news of this murderous attack spread like a
flame through the land.   In every State in the South
it found a ready response in the sullen passions of
the slave-owners, whose hatred for the Abolitionists it
exactly expressed.   Throughout the North it raised a
nobler sentiment, and called forth a resolve that the
system which placed millions of human beings under
the absolute power of such men as this Brooks must
be swept away.   In both North and South that blow
in the Senate House at Washington fell like a spark
among the stubble : it set the nation on fire.

Among others who denounced the shameful deed was
young Garfield.   The students of his university called
a public meeting to protest against the crime, and
Garfield was the principal speaker.   His address more
than surprised his companions.   All the passionate

vehemence of his mighty heart was awakened by this outrage, and all the slumbering hatred which he had nursed since boyhood against the abominations of slavery sprang to his lips.

As his hot words swept over the audience, his fellow-students sat amazed. Great as had been their belief in his powers, they had hardly expected this, and they heard enough that night to convince them that one of the mighty men of the earth was rising up amongst them; and they went away from the meeting whisper ing, " We have heard great things to-day."

CHAPTER XIV.

THE FIRST BLOW.

GARFIELD was twenty-six when he left Williams' University. He entered this college a raw student from a Western seminary ; he left it a distinguished scholar, a graduate with honours, and a popular lay preacher and platform speaker.

In spite of many flattering offers, he had remained true to the Western Institute at Hiram. Before his return he was appointed teacher of ancient languages and literature there, and to this office he came full of enthusiasm.

The salary was only one hundred and fifty pounds a year, less by one-third than the sum offered him by the trustees of the high school at Troy, but that made no difference to Garfield. He brought to the duties of his profession a profound love for the school to which he himself was so greatly indebted, and an ardent desire to help young fellows as poor as himself. He found plenty of scope for his gifts, and he taught with such success that in two years' time he was appointed principal of the Institution.

This was the height of his ambition. Around him were some three hundred young people, sons and daughters of the great West, whose mental and spiritual training was in his hands. He regarded it as a sacred trust, and he solemnly devoted his life to the service of these Western students.

His ideal was a high one. The teacher, he felt, was a builder of the nation, and he resolved that no work should leave his hands that was ill planned or badly done.

The memory of his own early struggles made him especially mindful of the poorer scholars, and his keen eye was always on the look-out for young men of promise. Perfectly free in his intercourse with the students, the young principal maintained his influence by the nobility of his character and the steadiness of his aim. His only wish was to help his pupils. And they believed in him with a faith that in the years to come transformed his classes into battalions on the field of battle.

The slavery question was still exercising the minds

of all parties when Garfield returned to Hiram. His power as a speaker made him an important ally to the Abolitionist party in his country, and his fame brought numberless demands for platform work. The Democratic party in the States had unhappily identified itself with slavery. Its leaders defended the system, its members voted in its favour; while the Republicans led the way for its abolition.

Soon after Garfield's return to Hiram, a well-known Democrat named Hart visited the town, to deliver an address on slavery. It was a clever speech, and made some impression, and the principal of the Institute was urged by the Republicans to reply. After some hesitation, Garfield did so. The answer was said to have been calmly given, but its grim facts of slavery horrors, its awful pictures of slavery evils, were so overwhelming, that his opponent was completely crushed.

This triumph naturally raised the demand that a man of such abilities should go into politics, and he was formally requested to become a candidate for the State Legislature. For a long time he refused. The interests of his school seemed so great, and his love for the work was so strong, that for a while nothing could move him.

In the year 1859, however, the appeals of his fellow-townsmen had grown so urgent, that he reluctantly

NEGROES STOLEN FROM THE WEST COAST OF AFRICA WERE
SOLD INTO SLAVERY.

became a candidate for the Senate of the State of Ohio. He had held back until the trustees of the Institute and his fellow-teachers joined their entreaties with the townsmen, and offered during his absence to do double duty in the school to release him for the public service. Greatly touched by these generous offers, Garfield at length consented, and was at once nominated a candidate to the parliament of his native State.

Though he had been slow to accept nomination, he did not hold back when once the battle had begun, and some few who looked with doubt on his youth and in-experience soon found that they had in their midst a bold though prudent leader. He won the seat by a large majority, and entered the Senate in the month of January 1860.

The United States of America consisted then of thirty-eight States and ten Territories. Each State is governed by its own parliament, which consists of a House of Senate and a House of Representatives. The whole of these States and Territories are again united under a Federal Government, at the head of which is the President of the United States. Each State sends to the Federal Government two Senators and from one to thirty Representatives, according to its population.

The State of Ohio, in whose Senate Garfield took his seat for the first time, is considerably larger than

Ireland, and contains a more numerous population. It was organised into a State and admitted into the Union in 1803.   Its population then was less than fifty thousand.   Twenty years afterwards it had become ten times as great, and at the time of Garfield's election to its Senate, numbered nearly two and a half millions.

Garfield had won his spurs as a politician in the discussion of the slavery question, and very soon he was called to give practical form to his opinions.   For years there had been a conviction among many of the people of the Northern States that slavery was wrong, that it was a crime against man and a sin against God. The Southern States where slavery existed defended the institution without shame and without fear.   They bitterly resented any discussion of the subject by the North, and they took effectual means to suppress any adverse opinions in the South.

In the very year of Garfield's election, nearly a thousand white persons in the slave States were robbed, whipped, imprisoned, tarred and feathered, or murdered, on suspicion of sympathy with the slaves.

New and bitter laws were passed in the Southern States against teaching or helping the negroes; and in several States it was calmly proposed to deprive the free blacks also of their liberty, to sell them back into bondage in order to raise money for the support of the elementary schools.   In defiance of the laws of

the Federal Government, the slave trade also was
reintroduced, and negroes stolen from the West
Coast of Africa were once more landed and sold into
slavery.

This open and insolent growth of the spirit of slavery
in the South was slowly rousing the rest of the great
nation from its slumber. Statesmen had been silent
too long, politicians and preachers had apologised for
the evil, and the people as a whole had given no sign,
until provoked by those flagrant attempts to carry the
vile system into those newer parts of the country called
Territories, vast districts of only partly occupied land
which had not yet been erected into States.

Then the controversy became sharp and bitter, and
the men of the North began to speak out. To the
younger men especially was the system hateful, and it
was plain that in the free States a new generation had
risen up which was prepared to wash its hands of the
curse of slavery. Some of the Southern States, afterwards known as the Confederates, formed themselves
into an association, and threatened to withdraw from
the Federal Union; and civil war between the slave
States and the free was by the more thoughtful and far-
seeing deemed inevitable.

The young Senator Garfield was one of the first to
realise the true position of affairs. During his first
year in the State Senate he had made his mark, in the

next he became by the mere force of his character and the intensity of his feelings its leader.

The President of the United States at the time was James Buchanan, a Democrat and a friend of the slave-owners. He, with others in high places, seemed bent on giving the South every opportunity to strengthen itself against the North.

In many of the Northern States, it was hoped by the timid that war could be averted by passing laws which would please the South. But Garfield knew better. He saw that war must come, and he urged his friends to be prepared. One night he said to a fellow-Senator, Cox, who shared his lodgings, "Cox, war is inevitable."

"It is, as sure as you live," was the reply.

Then said Garfield, " If it comes, you and I must fight ; let us then pledge our lives to our country in her hour of peril." And standing there, these two men, grand types of the Young America which was rising above the shame of its dark past, pledged themselves to fight for the old flag and for human right.

Abraham Lincoln succeeded Buchanan in the Presidency of the United States, and the Confederates withdrew from the Union, and elected a friend of the slave-owners, named Jefferson Davis, as their President. Then the first blow was struck. At Charleston was a stronghold called Fort Sumter, which commanded the

THE DEFENCE OF FORT SUMTER.

bay and harbour. The fort was held by Major Anderson for the Federal Government. The garrison was small, consisting only of some seventy men, who were without provisions.

The Confederates demanded possession of the fort. Anderson held out for a day or two, until the walls were beaten down about his ears, and then surrendered the fortress to the rebels. This was the beginning of war.

The news of the victory was flashed through the land, and the nation stood aghast, to find that the Great Rebellion had begun.

CHAPTER XV.

DARK DAYS FOR THE UNION.

President Lincoln's Appeal to the Country — Dark Days for the Northern States—A Decisive Battle—Glorious News.

HE question of slavery was the real cause of the American Civil War, though in the first instance the object of the North was solely to save the Union. Six of the slave States had withdrawn from the Union. They had appointed as their President Jefferson Davis, and had attempted to seize all the arms and forts within the border of the States.

The ease with which Fort Sumter had fallen into their hands encouraged them to believe that they could easily snap the bonds which held the Union together. In the South the white population was supposed to be far superior to their Northern neighbours in all the arts of war.

Their position as slave-masters had bred in them an

arrogant temper and a reckless spirit. They were more practised at the rifle, better used to horsemanship, and more familiar with field sports, than the men of the North. And they fondly boasted that one Virginian could beat five Yankees.

Indeed, the Southern States were so confident of their strength, that they did not really believe the North would fight; they might protest, they said, but that would be all.

But men who talked like this little understood the intense love of country which burned in Northern hearts. The moment Fort Sumter fell, Lincoln appealed to the country for seventy-five thousand soldiers, and within three days nearly a hundred thousand men had volunteered.

Then the war dragged slowly on for four long, weary years.

At first the tide of battle ran full against the Federals. Their first victory had encouraged the rebels. Then a battle of very much more importance was fought close to a stream known as Bull's Run, and here again the North was defeated. Then others joined the Confederates.

Several of the most brilliant soldiers and commanders, such as Lee and Jackson, were Virginians and slave-holders, and these of course threw in their lot with the South, and for some time the North had no men of equal capacity to set against them. Thus for months and almost years it seemed as if the Confederates would succeed, and that the fetters of the slave would be fixed more firmly than ever.

But defeat and delay were in reality making leaders for the North. A young engineer officer named M'Clellan was put in command at first. His appointment appeared to be a fortunate one. He speedily organised and placed in the field a splendid army, and it was fondly expected that a few months with such troops as his would end the war. But M'Clellan, though a brave soldier and an able man, was a disappointment. Like the father of Frederick the Great, he was an ideal drill-master, but an indifferent general. He was afraid to risk his magnificent army, and while he dallied his foes snatched victory after victory.

Those were dark days for the Northern States, yet through the darkness they did not falter. They felt that their cause was just, and they were prepared to suffer and die for it. At the head of the State was the great and noble Lincoln, whose calm and indomitable spirit was unbroken under the heaviest disaster.

On the first of July 1863, General Lee, who had invaded Pennsylvania with an army of seventy thousand men, advanced upon the little town of Gettysburg.

Here he met and partially defeated the Federal troops under General Meade. Meade had entrenched himself on the hill above the town; but, though defeated, he was not dislodged. The second day a further attack was made, and once more the Federals suffered heavy losses. Part of their position was carried, and Lee believed that another day would give him such a victory as would place the whole of the Northern States with all their wealth at his feet.

It was a terrible moment for the North. The fate of the Union and of the nation depended on that battle; and when, at the close of the second day's struggle, the news was flashed by telegraph through the length and breadth of the land, that Meade was again defeated, a great gloom and sorrow hung over the Northern States. At Washington, the Government sat in terror. In hundreds of churches and thousands of homes throughout the land, the wives and children of the soldiers spent the night in prayer.

At length the fateful day dawned, and the two armies met once more. Under cover of the darkness, Meade had been quietly strengthening his position, and when the sun rose over the camp, it was seen that once more he was ready to face his hitherto victorious enemy.

The battle began at noon. For some time the result was uncertain. Then for a third time the Confederates began to make headway, and it is said that some of Lee's generals actually congratulated him upon a final victory. But the battle was not ended.

The Federals had their backs to the wall, and the dogged determination which is the strength and glory of the Yankee character showed itself at last.

Again and again the best troops of the Confederate army dashed up the slope of the low hill, only to break against the stubborn bands of men who could die but would not be defeated. And when at length the rebels made one more terrible rush, they were met, hurled back, broken, beaten, and scattered, and the battle was over.

That night, the Fourth of July, the anniversary of the Declaration of American Independence, there went up a shout through the North and East that must have reached to heaven. Just outside the town of Richmond, in Virginia, was a huge prison. Here some hundreds of Northern officers, prisoners of war, were held in captivity. They had heard of the struggle going on at Gettysburg, and they knew how much depended on that battle.

When, after the first and second days' fighting, the news of the Federal repulses reached them, their hearts sank. Eagerly yet anxiously they waited for the morrow. No eye in that dreary building was closed that night in sleep. The morning of the fourth day rose. They waited in fear, and strange rumours reached them. Some one brought word that their brethren were again defeated, and tears of shame and sorrow ran down many a worn face.

Then an aged negro approached the prison. He brought wonderful news, and through the bars he conveyed tidings of the Federal victory. For a moment the good news was scarcely believed. Next loud sobs were heard, mingled with murmured praises; then suddenly from hundreds of lips there rose this glorious battle-song of the North, for they felt, though many a battle was to follow, that the Union was saved:—

BATTLE HYMN OF THE REPUBLIC.

"Mine eyes have seen the glory of the coming of the Lord,
He is trampling out the vintage where the grapes of wrath are stored;
He hath loosed the fateful lightning of His terrible swift sword:
His Truth is marching on.

"I have seen Him in the watch-fires of a hundred circling camps;
They have builded Him an altar in the evening dews and damps;
I have read His righteous sentence by the dim and flaring lamps:
His day is marching on.

"I have read a fiery gospel writ in burnished rows of steel,
  'As ye deal with My contemners, so with you My grace
      shall deal;'
  Let the Hero born of woman crush the serpent with His heel
          Since God is marching on.

"In the beauty of the lilies Christ was born across the sea,
  With a glory in His bosom that transfigures you and me;
  As He died to make man holy, let us die to make men free,
          While God is marching on."

CHAPTER XVI.

Ulysses S. Grant—Recruits from all Classes—Senator Garfield appointed Colonel of a Regiment—Asking for Guidance.

HE Union was saved, but the struggle was not over. During the earlier years of the war the strong men of the North had been slowly coming to the front. One of these was a stubborn, silent soldier named Grant, who, after an early training as a military cadet, and some experience in the Mexican war, had settled down to a clerkship in a leather shop in Illinois.

When war broke out, Ulysses S. Grant recruited a regiment of Illinois men, of which he was made commander, and then entered upon that military career which at length ranked him among the two or three greatest soldiers of the age, and finally placed him in the presidential chair.

8

To General Grant more than to any man belongs the honour of the triumph of the Federal armies.   But Grant was strong because of the innate nobleness of the men he commanded, and the magnificent steadfastness of the people who supported him.   That support was given with a liberal hand.   Probably never since the days when the people of Israel stripped themselves of their jewels to build the tabernacle, did a nation contribute of their treasures so eagerly and whole-heartedly as the American nation at this crisis.

Private individuals subscribed vast sums of money, teachers of schools voluntarily gave up a fixed proportion of their salary, churches and societies made regular collections, farmers carried their produce into the camps, and women devoted their skill to nursing the sick and wounded.

The highest honour that men could claim was to serve in the ranks of the army ; and rich and poor alike shouldered the musket and slept side by side upon the field of battle.

On one occasion the money which was needed for the pay of a New England regiment was delayed, and it was feared that the families of the soldiers, as well as the soldiers themselves, might in consequence be placed in distress.   Elias Howe, the inventor of the sewing-machine, who was serving as a private in the ranks, stepped forward, pulled out his cheque-book, and wrote on the spot a cheque for £20,000, which he handed to his colonel for the use of his comrades.

The army was composed not only of the strongest, but also of the noblest men of the nation. Ministers led their congregations into battle. Teachers gathered their young men together, and went with them to fight for the country; and among the first of these, James Garfield, the young principal of the Hiram Institute, marched at the head of a hundred students of his college, and with their help gained the earliest victory of the Federal army.

When Fort Sumter fell, Lincoln, as we have seen, appealed at once for 75,000 volunteers. The call, which was read in the various States, was heard in the Senate of Ohio, of which Garfield was a member. The moment that the President's message had been read, Garfield rose to his feet, and moved that Ohio should contribute 20,000 men and about a million of money to the war. The motion was received and passed with the heartiest approval, and the young Senator was at once appointed to serve in the new army.

He raised two regiments, of one of which he was made colonel. This was work in which he had had no previous experience; yet he soon proved himself a master of the business. Commander, officers, and privates were all alike, raw recruits; but Garfield soon drilled both himself and his men into shape.

As a skilled carpenter, he could handle a workman's tools. He made a number of models and blocks, and with these he studied the art of war. Then he taught his officers as he used to teach his classes; and so, by sticking to his old principles of "thorough," he soon produced a regiment second to none in the Northern army. Garfield's duty in the first place was to help to keep the State of Kentucky out of the hands of the Confederates. At Middle Creek on January 10th, and again on the 17th at Prestonburg, he defeated General Marshall. In his regiment he had a number of his own Hiram boys, over whom he watched as an elder brother. The affection of the young men for their friend and teacher was unbounded, and with him to lead them there were few perils from which they shrank.

Garfield had not taken up the trade of a soldier for pleasure or for personal ambition, but out of a stern sense of duty. Brave and resolute as he was, he was still more remarkable for the genuine kindness and even tenderness of his nature. Before going into the war, he was deeply concerned for his mother and for his wife and child. If his life were taken, there was no provision for these dear ones. The night, therefore, he volunteered, he took his mother's Bible and sat down to read, determined to let the voice of God speak to him on this momentous matter.

He had not long to wait. As he read and meditated, he could hear one solemn voice speaking all the time in his heart, like the voice which fell upon the ear of the Hebrew captain, bidding him go forward to fight, as he said, for his country and for human right.

CHAPTER XVII.

WINNING HIS SPURS.

The Hiram Boys in Action—Terrible Odds—A Daring Deed—A Ride
for Life—Major-General Garfield.

HE period of Garfield's active service in the army was a little over two years; yet in that short time he rose from lieutenant-colonel to major-general, and performed some deeds of valour that will never be forgotten. Within three months of raising his regiment, he was prepared to take the field, and the sphere of his operations was the State of Kentucky.

This large and important State, which lay on the borders of the slave-holding districts, was by no means unanimous in favour of the Union. General Marshall, with an army of 5000 Confederates, had taken up a position in Eastern Kentucky; and Garfield, having reported himself to General Buell at Louisville, was ordered to march against the invaders. It

GARFIELD AND HIS REGIMENT
GOING INTO ACTION.

was at Middle Creek where the two small opposing armies met. Garfield's forces numbered, all told, about 2600; the Confederates were nearly double. Garfield found the enemy posted on the double crest of a low hill, and he at once commenced his attack.

The charge was led by the hundred Hiram students, who were ordered to cross the stream and climb the opposite ridge, the intention being to draw the enemy out of their ambuscade. But the slope of the hill was swept with rebel bullets, and the Hiram boys had to seek shelter among the trees.

While the young men held their position in the timber, a support of 500 men came up, and the little brigade faced nearly 4000 muskets. Then Colonel Moore and his loyal Kentuckians volunteered to carry the hill. Standing on a rock in full sight of his men, and a conspicuous mark for the Confederates' rifles, Garfield directed the fight. For a while it seemed doubtful on which side victory should fall, until through the trees the commander caught sight of a glancing banner, and with a shout he announced that reinforcements had arrived. The enemy had seen it also, and at once began a retreat, which soon became a scamper.

For this brilliant little victory, the first that had fallen to the Federal arms, Garfield was made a brigadier-general. He was now thirty-one years of age, and had served in the army about four months.

Garfield's force in Eastern Kentucky held the field, but they held it starving. Their provisions were done, the roads were impassable, the people unfriendly, and the river swollen and dangerous. But Garfield's early experience as a canal boy now stood him in good stead. Among his troops was his old companion and humble friend of the towpath, Harry S. Brown, the poor fellow who, in spite of a good heart and shrewd sense, had been so long the unhappy victim of intemperance. But the man adored his young officer, and now, at a critical moment in Garfield's career, Brown was able to render him and the good cause an important service.

The army was encamped near the scene of its victory. Close by was the Big Sandy river, a deep and rapid and swollen stream. No local boatman would venture down the torrent at such a time. And yet that was the sole direction from which the little army might expect supplies.

Garfield sent for Harry Brown, who had been acting as scout. The two sprang into a skiff, and succeeded in descending the river. At Catletsburg, on the mouth of the Big Sandy, they found a little old-fashioned steamer belonging to a Confederate, and of this vessel they took possession. The steamer was loaded with provisions, and Garfield assumed command. It was in vain that the rebel captain protested, and explained the terrors of the passage. He had to do with a man whose spirit of duty completely lifted him above the sense of fear.

For two days and nights Garfield stood at the helm of the vessel, and battled with the swollen torrent. More than once they were aground, but the resolute management of Garfield and the unflinching obedience of Harry the scout surmounted every difficulty, and at length the little steamer came puffing in sight of the almost despairing camp.

The men were beside themselves with joy; they shouted and sang and danced, and declared that with such a leader there was no danger they would not face.

But it was at the battle of Chickamauga that Garfield's most daring feat was performed. In the early part of 1863 he was made chief of the staff to General Rosecrans, and in this capacity organised his famous corps of scouts. The summer and autumn were spent in opposing General Bragg, one of the ablest of the Southern commanders. On the 19th and 20th of September the battle of Chickamauga was fought. The right division of the army, under the immediate direction of Rosecrans, was cut in two by Bragg. As the Federals began their retreat, Garfield, who chafed bitterly under this repulse, begged permission to ride back to the second column of the army, which was under the command of General Thomas. He hoped to reach this division, and encourage the general to continue the battle until Rosecrans could collect his broken forces and entrench himself in Chattanooga.

Great as was the need, Rosecrans hesitated before allowing Garfield to run the risk of such a ride. At length he reluctantly consented. Grasping Garfield's hand, his chief said, "We may not meet again. Good-bye; God bless you." And, with this kindly farewell in his ears, the young brigadier - general rode away.

With three companions for guides, he made for the tangled forest. Then they trotted past Rossville. Here, as they swept along the narrow road, a thousand rifles opened fire upon them, and two of the little party fell. They had ridden into a body of Confederate skirmishers who were hanging upon the flank of Thomas's army.

Garfield put his horse to the fence and leaped into a cottonfield. The hedge on the other side of the field was lined with muskets. Garfield rode a zig-zag course across the field, and so prevented the enemy from taking aim. His course slanted upwards, and he knew that if he could but gain the top of the hill, he would be out of range of the rebel rifles. Twice a volley was fired, and the second time his horse received a nasty flesh wound ; but still Garfield was uninjured. His good horse, though losing blood fast, kept on. He had reached the crest of the hill just as the second volley of bullets whizzed past him, and the next moment he was safe. A party of Thomas's troops rode out to meet him, they dashed down the hill together, and in a few more minutes Garfield's horse dropped dead at the feet of General Thomas.

But the object of his ride was accomplished. Thomas held out long enough to enable Rosecrans to strengthen himself and occupy Chattanooga, and the army was saved. The stand which General Thomas made at Chickamauga was said to be the most brilliant defence of the whole war, and the ride of Garfield the most heroic deed. For this exploit he was raised to the rank of major-general.

CHAPTER XVIII.

Called to Washington—Elected to the Congress—His Plan for increasing the Army—The Slaves' Friend—Abraham Lincoln shot—Stilling the Tumult.

AFTER the battle of Chickamauga, General Garfield retired from the army. His help was greatly needed in a sphere where the same courage would find scope, but where other gifts besides decision and dash were required.

He had been a State Senator for Ohio for several years. Now he was to become a Member of Congress, the national Parliament of the United States.

He was elected a representative of Congress in 1862, but did not immediately take his seat. So far, his place seemed with the army; but when, in 1863, immediately after the battle of Chickamauga, he went with despatches to Washington, President Lincoln expressed a strong desire that he should remain, and help to guide the affairs of the war in the national Parliament. Such help as his was needed. Lincoln was beset by timid and divided, and in some cases interested, advisers, and the presence of a strong, fearless counsellor, as wise and experienced as Garfield, was a great accession of strength.

Here his moral courage was soon put to the test. More soldiers were urgently required, and two plans were laid before the country. One was to offer a bounty to volunteers; the other plan was to pass a law requiring every able-bodied man between the ages of eighteen and forty-five to be enrolled.

Garfield's party favoured the former plan. Garfield himself approved the latter. He said that, in such times as these, only the most worthless men would want to be bought, the best would feel it a duty to serve their country, and his vote was given in favour of compulsory enlistment. It was a step that required courage, for it placed him in opposition to the whole of his friends and supporters. But he said, " I must vote according to conscience. My constituents may refuse to elect me again, but for fear of that, I cannot trample on my convictions." By his eloquence he was able to carry the law calling out half a million of men, and it was not long before he convinced the whole country, as he had convinced Congress, of the wisdom of his advice.

Garfield had long ago discovered that it was almost as dangerous to refuse his friends as to oppose his foes. But the straight and simple line he had marked out for himself was his sufficient guide. There was one man, he used to say, from whose company he could never escape. He must eat, walk, work, and sleep with him; and no matter whom he disappointed besides, he was bound to gain and keep the respect of that one individual, who was himself. It was a wholesome saying, and it expressed the principles which guided all his public life.

While the war lasted, no man more resolutely opposed any kind of concession to the rebels; but when it was ended, he was foremost in his attempts to soothe the passions which the war had enkindled.

From one point, however, he never flinched; that was in the treatment of the negroes. He had begun his career as their advocate, he continued it as their protector and friend. When an officer on service, he had risked his position, and even his life, by refusing to surrender a poor fugitive slave who had sought shelter in his camp, although ordered to do so by his superior officer. And when, at the close of the war, a bill was brought before Congress to limit the rights of the freed slaves, Garfield indignantly and successfully opposed it.

On the 14th of April 1865, just after being elected

to the Presidency for the second time, Abraham
Lincoln was shot by a rebel sympathiser, named Booth.
And the same night the life of the Secretary of State,
Seward, was also attempted. These crimes roused the
people of the North to madness. In every city the
men assembled with ominous cries for vengeance.

In New York, a foolish man called out that Lincoln
ought to have been shot long ago. That cruel speech
cost the speaker his life. He was struck down by a
hundred hands. Then a vast crowd gathered in front
of the *World* newspaper office, which was a supporter
of the rebels. It was a crisis when a single spark
might kindle a fire that only could be put out by
bloodshed. At that moment a man stepped out upon
the balcony of the City Hall,—a tall, portly man, whose
mighty voice was heard above the tumult of the
crowd of angry men. There was stillness, and then,
solemnly and slowly, the voice cried, " Fellow-citizens,
—Clouds and darkness are round Him! His pavilion
is on the dark waters, and thick clouds of the skies!
Justice and judgment are the habitation of His throne!
Mercy and truth shall go before His face! Fellow-
citizens, God reigns, and the Government at Washington
still lives!" As the angry waves of Galilee were hushed
at the sound of the voice of Christ, so did the surging
passion of that great multitude grow still at the words
of His servant that day. Men ceased from cries of

vengeance, and turned to Him who "had made His throne in the heavens," and bowed their hearts before Him.

The voice which swayed and stilled the crowd that day was the voice of Garfield; he it was who, in that dreadful moment, stood in the gap between the living and the dead.

CHAPTER XIX.

Statesman and Citizen—Leader of the House of Representatives—
Elected President—The Secret of Success—Struck down by an
Assassin—Hovering between Life and Death—Death and Burial.

ARFIELD'S life, above that of most men, was given to the world as a splendid example of perfect integrity and manly independence. All through that romantic career this had been its most remarkable feature. His talents were great, his powers of endurance were great, his energy and courage were great; but his love of right was greater and grander than all.

From that moment when he awoke to a true sense of his responsibilities as a servant of God, he began to fit himself for all the duties of man. For whatever duty claimed his service he was found prepared; and when the call came suddenly to the kingly seat, and then yet more swiftly to the martyr's crown, he was still found ready. Dividing his time between Congress at

Washington and his little home farm at Mentor, he served his nation as a statesman, and ruled his happy household as a citizen.

His noble mother, by whose godly counsel he had walked, spent some happy years in his home; while his brave and loving wife cheered and helped and inspired him in those days of patient service.

Gradually he gained the position of Leader of the House of Representatives. In 1879 he was elected Senator of the United States; and then, quite unexpectedly, in the following year he was lifted into the highest place of all.

The President of the United States is elected every four years. In each State a number of persons known as "electors" are chosen by the votes of the people. The number of these electors is exactly the same as the number of the Representatives of each State. These persons then meet and elect the President and Vice-President for the ensuing four years. The great and dignified office of President is the summit of an American's ambition; and it is only in the United States that a poor lad may hope and believe it possible for him to climb from the humblest position to a rank which places him on an equality with kings.

Long before the time for election, the great parties in the State select their candidates for this high office. Garfield belonged to the Republican party, and the people chiefly opposed to him were called Democrats. Previous to the Presidential election, the leading men of the party met in a vast hall at Chicago to decide upon a candidate. Several names were proposed, but it was found at first impossible to select one man upon whom all the delegates of the Republican party could agree.

Thirty-five times a ballot had been taken, and they seemed no nearer than before. But at the thirty-fifth it was found that one name had received about fifty votes. When that name was read, it was greeted with a mighty cheer, which grew louder and louder, until the whole of the vast building resounded with the name of James A Garfield. Another ballot was taken, and Garfield was found to be the chosen of his party.

He was nominated as the Republican candidate; and on November 2, 1880, the "little sapling" of the Western Reserve became the President of the United States, the uncrowned monarch of one of the greatest nations of the world. Thus had he marched along. At fourteen he was working at the carpenter's bench; at sixteen he was a canal boatman; two years later he entered the Chester school; at twenty-one he was a common school teacher.

Then in his twenty-third year he entered the university, graduating three years afterwards. At twenty-

MRS. JAMES GARFIELD.

seven he became principal of the Hiram Institute. The next year he was a Member of the Ohio Senate. At thirty-one he was at the head of a regiment; at thirty-two, a major-general; at thirty-three, a Member of Congress; at forty-eight he was made a Member of the National Senate; and at fifty he became President of the United States.

We have said that the secret of Garfield's success was his integrity. To this he owed the respect which advanced him to each position of trust until it made him head of the Government. And it was to this noble quality of his character that he owed his death. Corruption had grown up in connection with the offices of State, and Garfield's last mission was to purge the Government of this taint. He was resolved to set his face against "the waste of time and the obstruction to public business caused by the greedy crowd of office-seekers." And he also announced that "rigid honesty and faithful service would be required from every officer of the State."

This conduct bitterly annoyed some of his own party, who had expected that Garfield would follow the example of other Presidents, and turn out all the civic officers, to make room for his own friends. This annoyance at length found expression in the wicked act of a wretched creature, a disappointed office-seeker, named Guiteau.

The new President had been but a few months in office, when Guiteau followed him into the railway station at Washington, and, as he entered the waiting-room, shot him in the back. The President fell wounded, but not unconscious. In great pain, he still remembered his loved ones, and moaned, "My poor wife and children." Then he dictated a message to his wife.

A struggle with death ensued, on which the whole world looked with awe.

For weeks the President hovered between life and death, showing ever the same sublime spirit of cheerful patience and Christian resignation which had adorned his life. At length the end came, and on the 19th of September 1881 he fell asleep. His body was removed to Washington, where he was laid in state. On the bier a wreath of white roses rested, bearing the simple inscription—"From Queen Victoria to the memory of the late President Garfield, an expression of her sorrow, and her sympathy with Mrs. Garfield and the American nation."

Through that room passed a hundred and thirty thousand persons of all ranks, to take one last look at the man whose life had been so great, and whose dying had been so glorious. Then in the cemetery of his native Cleveland, James A. Garfield was laid to rest.

The spontaneous affection of his countrymen amply provided for his beloved family; and his martyrdom, it

was said, did more than any other event could have
done to draw the North and South together.   His death
was mourned, and the manner of it hated by every
section and party alike, and the whole nation, united
now in sorrow, bowed in loving tenderness over the
grave of one of its greatest children.

CHAPTER XX.

ONE of the pleasantest things in the story of Garfield is the devotion of friends and companions, which followed and helped him all his life. To an orphan lad, the son of a poor widow in the backwoods of the State of Ohio, there seemed little chance of greatness; and yet out of that poor cabin in the woods, in which sat the weeping mother and her four fatherless children, came one who was destined to stand among princes.

It was the self-denial of his mother, elder brother, and sister which made it possible for James Garfield to rise. When the father died suddenly, leaving his family on the comparatively new clearing, Thomas, the eldest son, became the manager of the farm. "I can plough and plant, mother. I can sow the wheat too, and cut the wood, milk the cows, and do heaps of thing for you."

THE WHITE HOUSE.

This was the elder lad's answer to his mother's question, "Should they sell the farm now that her husband was dead?" and it decided her. And so the boy-farmer commenced his labours, and mother and children toiled together in humble and happy love.

But though Thomas was compelled to work, he was determined that his baby brother should have an education. And when a school was opened some distance off, he resolved that "Jimmy" must be one of the scholars. But how was a lad of four to get to school nearly two miles away. The answer came from a devoted sister, who said, "I'll carry him"; and the good, brave girl, with a homely name and a noble heart, trudged the long distance day by day, with a little sister at her side, and a little brother on her back. And that was how, aided by loving hands and loyal hearts, little James Garfield, the future professor, and general, and President of the United States, began his career.

You remember how Thomas, with all his duties and responsibilities about the farm, yet found a little time on his hands to do odd jobs for a neighbour, and so obtain a little money.

When he came home with his first earnings, he walked straight up to his mother, laid it down in her lap, and said, "Now the shoemaker can come and make Jimmy a pair of shoes." What a splendid fellow

Thomas was! He seemed to have no thought for himself, but only to be wearing out his young life for
others.   Surely in the long hereafter, when they reckon
up the good deeds in each life, the reaping of this little
backwoods' farmer will be a glorious one, for he sowed a
mighty harvest of love.

One story of this dear brother should never be forgotten.   His brother James slept on the floor of the
loft beside him, and the restless little fellow would kick
off the blankets a dozen times in a night.   Then, half
awake, he would say, "Tom, cover me up"; and the
patient hand, that never tired of helping others, would
replace the clothing, and the little head would sink
down again on its hard pillow.

Five-and-twenty years afterwards, when at the head
of an army, and after a great battle, he lay down on the
battlefield to sleep.   An officer heard him say, "Tom,
cover me up."   A friendly hand drew the blanket over
his shoulder, and awoke him by the act.   On being told
of his saying, General Garfield sat a moment silent, then
he told his comrades how he had been helped at home,
and all through life; and as he spoke of this brother's
love, his heart grew too full, and he turned aside and
wept.

Surely if there is one lesson more than another to
learn from the story of this splendid life, it is to be
found in the sacrifice of this elder brother, who, like

Jonathan of old, stepped aside and lent a hand that another should climb over his head.

Garfield was like David. His was the magnetic soul that drew all men to him, and then drew forth the best and brightest impulses of their natures.

THE END.

PRINTED BY MORRISON AND GIBB LIMITED, EDINBURGH

THE NATIONAL SUNDAY SCHOOL UNION

2/= net.
(Uniform with this Volume.)

THE SPLENDID LIVES SERIES

A Collection of Lives of Great Men and Women who have helped to make the world brighter and better.

Each Vol. crown 8vo, cloth boards, well illustrated.

57 & 59 LUDGATE HILL, LONDON, E.C. 4